Rookie reader®

Messy Bessey

Written by
Patricia and Fredrick McKissack

Illustrated by Dana Regan

Children's Press®
A Division of Grolier Publishing
New York • London • Hong Kong • Sydney
Danbury, Connecticut

To Mom Bess who is *never* a mess
—P. and F. M.

Reading Consultants
Linda Cornwell
Coordinator of School Quality and Professional Improvement
(Indiana State Teachers Association)

Katharine A. Kane
Education Consultant
(Retired, San Diego County Office of Education and San Diego State Univers

Visit Children's Press® on the Internet at:
http://publishing.grolier.com

Library of Congress Cataloging-in-Publication Data
McKissack, Pat.
    Messy Bessey / written by Patricia and Fredrick McKissack ; illustrated by
Dana Regan. – [Rev.] ed.
        p. cm. – (Rookie reader)
    Summary: Bessey finally cleans up her messy room.
    ISBN 0-516-21650-3 (lib. bdg.)   0-516-27003-6 (pbk.)
    [1. Cleanliness Fiction. 2. Orderliness Fiction. 3. Behavior Fiction.] I.
McKissack, Fredrick. II. Regan, Dana, ill. III. Title. IV. Series.
PZ7.M478693Me 1999   99-22472
[E]—dc21   CIP

GROLIER
PUBLISHING   1 2 3 4 5 6 7 8 9 10 R 08 07 06 05 04 03 02 01 00 99

Look at your room, Messy Bessey.

3

See colors on the wall,

books on the chair,

toys in the dresser drawer,

and games everywhere.

Messy Bessey, your room is a mess.
See shoes on the bed,
coat on the floor,

socks on the table,
and your hat on the door.

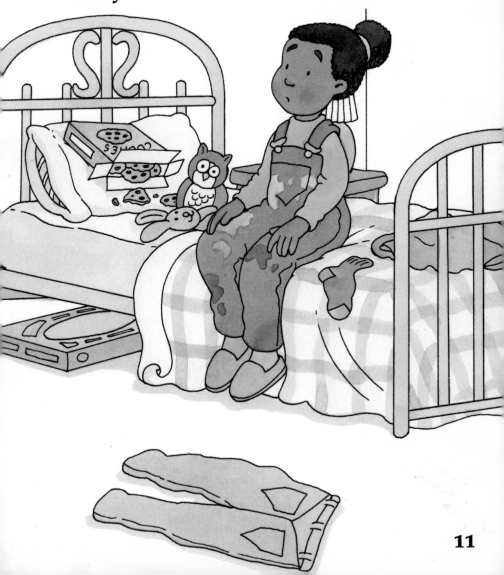

Bessey look at your messy room.
See the cup in the closet,

cookies on the pillow,

gum on the ceiling,
and jam on the window.

Messy, Messy Bessey,
your room is a mess.

17

Get the soap and water.
Get the mop and broom.

Get busy Messy Bessey.
You must clean your room.

So Bessey rubbed
and scrubbed the walls,

the ceiling,

and the floor.

She made her bed,

picked up her things,

and closed the closet door.

Hurrah!
Good for you Miss Bessey.
Just look at you, too.

Your room is clean and beautiful . . .

just like you!

Word List (70 words)

a	door	like	shoes
and	drawer	look	so
at	dresser	made	soap
beautiful	everywhere	mess	socks
bed	floor	messy	table
Bessey	for	Miss	the
books	games	mop	things
broom	get	must	too
busy	good	on	toys
ceiling	gum	picked	up
chair	hat	pillow	wall
clean	her	place	walls
closed	hurrah	please	water
closet	in	room	window
coat	is	rubbed	you
colors	jam	scrubbed	your
cookies	just	see	
cup	knock	she	

About the Authors

Patricia and Fredrick McKissack are freelance writers and editors, livi
in St. Louis County, Missouri. Their awards as authors include the Core
Scott King Award, the Jane Addams Peace Award, the Newbery Hon
and the 1998 Regina Medal from the Catholic Library Association.

The McKissacks have also written *Messy Bessey and the Birthα
Overnight*, *Messy Bessey's Closet*, *Messy Bessey's Garden*, *Messy Besse
Holidays*, and *Messy Bessey's School Desk* in the Rookie Reader series.

About the Illustrator

Dana Regan was born and raised in northern Wisconsin. She migrat
south to Washington University in St. Louis, and eventually to Kans
City, Missouri, where she now lives with her husband, Dan, and her son
Joe and Tommy.